SUFFOLK

ROBERT MALSTER

The fair comes to Framlingham, with roundabouts set up where medieval knights possibly honed their combat skills.

HISTORIC BRITAIN *from the Air*

SUFFOLK

ROBERT MALSTER

SUTTON PUBLISHING

First published in the United Kingdom in 1999 by
Sutton Publishing Limited · Phoenix Mill
Thrupp · Stroud · Gloucestershire · GL5 2BU

British Library Cataloguing in Publication Data
A catalogue record for this book is available from the British Library.

ISBN 0-7509-0802-5

Half-title page photograph: Giffords Hall, near Stoke-by-Nayland, with its red-brick gatehouse, dates from the reign of Henry VIII.
Title page: Castle Farm at Wattisham, a Victorian eccentric's 'Englishman's home'.

In memory of Pat Atfield
who died while this book was
in preparation

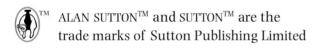
TM ALAN SUTTON TM and SUTTON TM are the
trade marks of Sutton Publishing Limited

Typeset in 11/14pt Photina.
Typesetting and origination by
Sutton Publishing Limited.
Printed in Great Britain by
The Bath Press, Bath.

Contents

The extensive railway layout within the works can be seen in this photograph of the British Sugar Corporation's factory at Ipswich, taken in 1968. The last of the engines used on these lines, a Peckett saddle-tank, was still working in the 1970s.

Introduction

Aerial photography, a product of the 20th century, has given us a new perspective on our history. After the Second World War, during which photographic reconnaissance missions carried out by the RAF proved invaluable in providing evidence of enemy activity in many fields, Prof. J.K.S. St Joseph and the Cambridge University Committee for Aerial Photography led the way in developing the use of similar techniques for archaeological studies and other research purposes.

Much earlier, during the First World War, Captain Waldon Hammond had participated in the development of aerial photography while at RAF Martlesham Heath, and some of the earliest photographs taken from aircraft show Ipswich and parts of the Suffolk countryside. At about the same time Charles Emeny was taking photographs from the air of his native Felixstowe, thanks to his friendship with pilots from the nearby Royal Naval Air Station.

Suffolk, which had seen the first stirrings of the use of aircraft for 'scouting' during the army manoeuvres of 1912, was therefore by no means left behind by the development of aerial photography. After the war Mr F.L. Wills, who had served as a photographer with the Royal Flying Corps, and pioneer flyer Claude Grahame-White saw the commercial possibilities of pictures taken from the air and set up Aerofilms, and photographs of Suffolk towns and villages were among the first to be taken by the company.

Those early photographs were taken using hand-held plate cameras which look incredibly cumbersome but produced some outstanding pictures. One photograph that has survived (and is reproduced on the cover of this book) shows F.L. Wills in the front cockpit of a hired de Havilland DH9, a type developed originally for military use during the First World War. The pilot, a Mr Shaw, occupies the middle cockpit and photographer Mr Freise-Green is in the rear cockpit with a massive plate camera.

The photographs that those men and their successors took show in some detail how Suffolk, its towns and villages have developed over the past 80 years. The first oblique photographs from 1920 show Ipswich as a market town retaining the street layout largely fixed in Anglo-Saxon times; others taken half a century later reveal a new road pattern being imposed on the old as building pushes out far beyond the confines of the old town.

In the countryside changes can be seen as the old field pattern is broken up to facilitate the use of larger machines and more efficient implements; new roads are driven across the old fields to accommodate the ever-increasing traffic; and along the coast the sea nibbles inexorably at the land, sometimes making dramatic inroads, as it did in 1953.

The pictures in this book have been carefully chosen from the vast Aerofilms library to illustrate as effectively as possible the changes that have come over Suffolk in the course of the 20th century, and to illustrate also aspects of history that have affected the appearance of the county in the more distant past. It is hoped they will indeed provide a new and enlightening perspective on Suffolk's long history.

At Sutton Hoo, across the Deben from Woodbridge, is the burial place of the Wuffinga dynasty who ruled East Anglia in what used to be termed the Dark Ages. In 1939 a fabulous treasure was found by archaeologists excavating a ship burial thought to have been that of Redwald, who died about 625 AD; the ship itself, almost 90 feet long, had been dragged more than a third of a mile and 100 feet up to the escarpment before being lowered into a trench already dug to receive it. That excavation, together with the various re-excavations and further investigations carried out since, shed a great deal of light on life and death in Anglo-Saxon England. This photograph, with east at the top, was taken on 11 April 1971 as a five-year re-excavation of the ship burial by a British Museum team under Rupert Bruce-Mitford was drawing to a close. The site of Mound 1, under which the ship burial was found, is clearly marked by white covers in the field at the top of the picture. Other mounds are visible in the same area. The features that appear rather like huge zip fasteners are trenches dug during the early part of the Second World War to prevent the landing of troop-carrying gliders.

Historical Sites

Elements of historic townscapes that have become fossilised over many centuries are plainly seen from the air. In this photograph of the Waveney Valley town of Bungay taken in 1972 the outline of the bailey of the castle founded by Roger Bigod in the 12th century stands out clearly in the street pattern, even though the ruins of the mighty stone keep are somewhat masked by the surrounding trees. Less prominent from the air, but the dominant building from ground level, is St Mary's Church at lower left.

The double banks and deep ditches of the Iron Age fort at Clare show up well in the autumn sunlight in this photograph taken in 1970. The area has never been investigated by excavation and the date of the earthworks remains uncertain, but the enclosure could have been inhabited around the time the Romans were occupying Britain.

During the 3rd century AD the Romans in Britain found themselves facing attack from raiders coming from the other side of the North Sea, and a series of forts was built along the east and south coasts as bases, both military and naval, to counter these attacks. Burgh Castle, close to the junction of the rivers Waveney and Yare and in Roman times at the side of a broad estuary, was probably one of the first of these forts to be built. The eastern wall and parts of the north and south walls can be seen in this photograph, looking north-east; the western wall is lost, but a line of bushes marks where it probably stood.

The powerful keep of Orford Castle, built by Henry II to defend the Suffolk coast and also to check the ambitions of the Bigods, one of whose castles was at Framlingham. It is polygonal – almost round – with three towers and a fore-building, and formerly had not only earthen embankments but curtain walls surrounding a considerable area. This view shows clearly some of the surviving earthworks, now marked by a network of paths. The building works of the 1160s cost £1413 9s. 2d – a massive sum when compared with the crown's average basic annual revenues at the time of under £10,000.

Framlingham Castle, seen here from the north-east, was the centre of administration for a great estate as well as a fortress from which the Bigod's challenged royal power. It represented a new concept in castle building which replaced the dominant keep of Orford with a strong curtain wall strengthened by a baker's dozen of towers. The curtain walls of about 1190 remain, but of the domestic buildings within nothing survives – the building inside the western wall is a poor-house built in 1729. Its size made possible the use of the castle as a base for an army, and in 1553 Queen Mary used it as such when the Duke of Northumberland attempted to put Lady Jane Grey, his daughter-in-law, on the throne.

The motte and bailey castle of Clare was the administrative centre of the Honour of Clare, a considerable collection of manors in the hands of Richard FitzGilbert, one of the Normans who came over with William the Conqueror. The family came to wield great power and influence, Gilbert de Clare marrying Joan of Acre, daughter of Edward I. Joan was buried in the grounds of the Augustinian priory founded by her husband in 1248; it can be seen at bottom left in the illustration. The priory was in private hands for many years, but since 1953 it has again been occupied by Austin Friars. The castle fell into decay and was considerably mutilated when the railway was constructed across the inner bailey in 1865. As can be seen in the photograph taken in 1953, the station was built within the ramparts of the old castle, with a goods shed and sidings at the foot of the still-impressive motte. The market place and the parish church lie just to the north, with Clare Common (the Iron Age fort illustrated earlier) further on. Even now the street pattern is influenced by the castle.

At Eye, too, the present-day street pattern betrays the extent of the Norman castle built by William Malet, another of the Conqueror's followers. The motte was from the late 17th to the early 19th century surmounted by a windmill, but this gave way to a mock stone keep which is in fact no more than a Victorian folly; it is possible that the original keep was of timber construction. The fine church of St Peter and St Paul with its striking 15th-century tower stands just to the east of the castle.

The great Abbey of St Edmund occupied a site on the west bank of the Lark; in this photograph taken in 1961 the ruins of this Benedictine establishment, once one of the half-dozen greatest and wealthiest in the country, can be seen exposed to view. As Professor J.K.S. St Joseph has said, few great abbeys have disappeared more completely, and the casual visitor can make little of the site, but from the air the extent of the abbey church can easily be appreciated. St James's Church, now the Cathedral, and the Norman tower which provided the main entrance to the abbey can be seen in the centre of the picture; the houses facing the tower, immediately south-east of the Cathedral, are built into the west end of the abbey church, and the white area towards the bottom of the picture marks the east end – altogether the church was some 500 feet long. Towards the top of the picture is the town of Bury St Edmunds, laid out by the 12th-century Abbot Anselm.

Leiston Abbey was founded by Ranulf de Glanville in 1182 on a site in the marshes bordering the coast, but that site proved inconvenient and perhaps unhealthy. In 1362 the abbey was moved further from the sea, some materials of the old buildings apparently being used in the new. Some of the buildings were destroyed by fire in 1389 and had to be rebuilt in 1388-89. This house belonged to the Premonstratensian order of 'White Canons' founded in 1120 at Prémontre in France. The canons adhered generally to the rule of St Augustine, but with additional austerities. The ruins were eventually absorbed into a farm, the farmhouse being built into the west end of the church and some of the abbey buildings becoming barns. It is now home to an organisation providing musical tuition for young people.

Kentwell Hall at Long Melford, built by the Clopton family in the mid-16th century, is a classic example of an Elizabethan house, constructed to an E-plan and with a moat more decorative than defensive. Seen in this view are the gardens at the rear of the house; not seen is the three-quarter-mile-long avenue of limes that was planted in 1678 leading from the Long Melford to Bury St Edmunds road. The estate had been acquired by the Cloptons through the marriage of Sir Thomas to Katherine Mylde not long before his death in 1383. Much more recently, in 1972, Patrick Phillips acquired the house, but not the estate, and proceeded to a long-term restoration of the house and recreation of the gardens. Historical re-enactments now attract many visitors to the house, including large numbers of schoolchildren who dress in their own version of Tudor costume and adopt new identities as servants or workers for the day.

Long Melford belonged to the Abbots of Bury St Edmunds from the reign of Edward the Confessor until at the Dissolution the last Abbot was forced to surrender it with all the abbey's other possessions to the King. Before very long the estate had come into the possession of a rising lawyer, William Cordell, and it was he who built the hall at about the same time that the Cloptons were building Kentwell; in 1578 Sir William's fortune was put to the test when he entertained Queen Elizabeth on one of her royal progresses. In this view one can see the extent of the gardens, which a plan of 1613 shows separated from the park by a wall and a moat; the western section of the moat still exists between the brick wall and the road. At the left is the octagonal Pavilion, a rare example of Tudor garden architecture. Melford Hall is now in the care of the National Trust, but it is still occupied by Sir Richard Hyde Parker, whose family came to the property in 1786.

Somerleyton Hall was a creation of Sir Morton Peto, railway contractor and builder, and the developer of 19th-century Lowestoft, who acquired the estate in 1844. The new hall built for Peto in the 1840s encased the original 17th-century building in a new one which Sir Nikolaus Pevsner describes as 'more Jacobean than any original Jacobean house.' The new design was carried out for him by the remarkable John Thomas, a sculptor-architect who had worked with Peto on the new Houses of Parliament. Peto subsequently laid out the gardens anew, with an elaborate parterre designed by William Andrews Nesfield which can be seen to good effect in this photograph taken in 1939.

Ickworth, built by Frederick Augustus Hervey, 4th Earl of Bristol and Bishop of Derry, is not easy to see from the ground as it hides behind the magnificent trees of the park; from the air it is seen in all its glory. The 104-foot rotunda was conceived as the living accommodation, the wings being intended to contain the Earl Bishop's art collections. To carry out his scheme he chose as architect Francis Sandys, who also built the Athenaeum at Bury St Edmunds, seen in the photograph on page 69. The Bishop, who achieved popularity in his diocese by helping Presbyterians and Roman Catholics alike, spent much of his time travelling abroad and never lived in the house he created.

The Countryside

Oulton Broad used to be described in the holiday brochures as the Gateway to the Broads. Formed, like the rest of the 'Norfolk Broads' – others besides Oulton are in Suffolk – by peat cutting in the early Middle Ages, Oulton Broad found itself playing a new role when Lowestoft harbour was constructed as part of a scheme to enable seagoing ships to sail upriver to Norwich. Lake Lothing, seen on the right of the 1969 photograph, was given an outlet to the sea, and a lock, almost in the middle of the picture, was built to take account of the different levels in the harbour and in the broad at various states of the tide. The yacht station, presided over at this time by a characterful former drifter skipper named Bill Soloman, can be seen packed with holiday craft on the freshwater side of the lock. In the middle distance on the right is the Brooke Marine shipyard, laid out in the early 1950s; one of the first orders was for 20 large trawlers for Russia, some of which appeared later at NATO naval exercises in the guise of electronics surveillance vessels.

Akenham is a tiny parish which in 1971 looked very much a peaceful rural community, for all that it now lies on the northern fringes of the town of Ipswich. In 1878, though, it was the scene of events that sparked a national scandal and led eventually to a change in the law relating to burials. Father George Drury, the Rector of nearby Claydon, who also had charge of Akenham, refused to read the burial service over the unbaptised two-year-old son of a Baptist farmworker, and broke up the nonconformist service held by a Dissenting minister on the field between the Hall Farm and the churchyard – an intended compromise arranged by the farmer, a friend and employer of the child's father. It was not the only time that the extreme cleric caused a stir in local church circles.

The network of dykes cut to drain Beccles Marshes shows up well in this view taken in 1963. The Beccles-Lowestoft railway line and the trackbed of the former Beccles to Yarmouth Southtown line, closed in 1959, cut across parts of the old field pattern. To the north is the Waveney. Windmills were employed to raise the water from the dykes into the river so as to drain many of the marshes, and when steam power arrived this sometimes replaced the mills; in 1882 an old beam engine and scoopwheel draining the Wheatacre marshes a few miles downriver were replaced by a horizontal compound engine by Holmes & Sons of Norwich driving a turbine pump capable of shifting 10,000 gallons a minute, and when the time came for the new engine to be set to work friends and neighbouring farmers were invited along to see the fun.

Cattawade, where road and railway cross the Stour side by side into Essex, was merely a hamlet of Brantham until the British Xylonite Company moved from Homerton, London, to a greenfield site astride the railway at Cattawade in 1887; almost overnight the population of Brantham soared from 440 to almost 700 as houses were built at Cattawade to accommodate the workers who moved from London. The pioneering plastics firm used both rail and sea transport to bring raw materials to the site. One of the road bridges had already in 1964 been replaced; the site of the former bridge, whose abutments can be seen in the photograph, is now occupied by a sluice.

Golding Constable, artist John's father, was miller at Flatford Mill, East Bergholt, and sent a lot of his flour down the Stour Navigation in barges to be exported to London. Today the mill no longer has the capacity to grind grain into flour but is a study centre to which people come to learn about the ecology of the Stour valley. In this 1961 photograph the mill is seen from the Essex side of the river, with the navigation channel running up to the lock, just visible among the trees at extreme left. Had the plans of the Eastern Counties Railway come to fruition in the 1840s the London–Ipswich line would have crossed the valley on a 70-foot high viaduct with about a hundred arches just yards above the mill; perhaps it is fortunate that when the Eastern Union built its line from Colchester to Ipswich in 1844–46 it was decided instead to cross the Stour on a low viaduct downriver at Cattawade.

The name Stoke usually implies either a suburb or a new settlement, but in the case of Stoke-by-Nayland it appears that Nayland is the junior partner, having been only a chapelry of Stoke. The village stands on a ridge above the valley of the Stour, and the 120-foot tower of St Mary's Church is a landmark for miles around. Constable drew it from the doorstep of a cottage across the road. Some of the old timber-framed houses are visible in the foreground, while towards the back of the picture are some of the village's newer homes, including a group of council houses in a close opening from the Leavenheath road.

Long Melford is another village, or small town, that grew prosperous on the woollen cloth trade. The magnificent Holy Trinity Church stands at the top of Melford Green, here in 1950 serving as temporary quarters for a fair; the showmen appear to be packing up their rides preparatory to leaving. The existing church, with its Lady Chapel projecting from the east end, is the result of a rebuilding between about 1460 and the end of the century, while the tower that complements the building so well is, believe it or not, a product of the early 20th century. The original tower had been lost in a fire and its replacement was lacking in stature, so George F. Bodley encased the 18th-century one in a new tower matching the scale and character of the 15th-century church.

The racecourse on Newmarket Heath has been the scene of many famous contests over the years and attracts a great throng of spectators. This view of the racecourse in 1949 shows that some of those who follow racing had by then taken to flying to the course in their own aircraft. During the Second World War the heath was used by the Royal Air Force, some of the personnel being accommodated in the stand, and the prototype of the RAF's first operational jet fighter, the Gloster Meteor, underwent taxiing trials there in 1942.

This view of the National Stud at Newmarket was taken in 1967, the year it was opened by the Queen. Built between 1963 and 1965 on 550 acres of agricultural land acquired from the Jockey Club, the National Stud is a commercial organisation owned by the nation and funded by the Horse Race Betting Levy Board. In the centre of the picture is the stallion unit with its archway, familiarly seen in press photographs of famous racehorses which have been retired to stud. The three circular buildings at bottom, mid-right and top are mare and foal units.

All Saints' Church at Wickhambrook, which contains features pointing to a Saxon foundation, stands in one corner of a very extensive parish. Settlement is spread over a number of scattered greens; Malting End can be seen along a winding road beyond the church, with Attleton Green in the distance. An early group of Dissenters who met for worship in various houses before they were able to set up their own chapel were responsible for one of the settlements gaining the name Meeting Green.

The wide-open landscape of the Fenland in the west of the county is well illustrated by this 1953 photograph of Bedford Farm, Mildenhall, with its large rectangular fields, fruit trees and bushes. Across the middle of the picture a watercourse wriggles its way, lined with trees and providing one of the few curves in a generally rectilinear view. In the background is Lakenheath airfield, employed during the Second World War as an RAF bomber base and later home to units of the US Air Force.

Some of the more modest gentlemen's houses had little impact on the landscape, their owners doing no more than carry on the same farming practices as their neighbours and not seeking to produce their own version of the countryside beyond the garden wall. Ashman's Hall at Barsham and Roos Hall, to the right of the above picture and within the boundaries of Beccles, are typical of this type, even if Ashman's Hall does have its miniature park on one side. The more affluent owners of houses such as Redgrave Hall, seen on the opposite page in a photograph taken in 1932, on the other hand, sought to produce their own artificial landscape in the form of an extensive park, sometimes moving a village to facilitate their 'landscaping'. At Redgrave, once the park of Bury Abbey and then the home of Lord Keeper Bacon, the owner went to Capability Brown for a landscaping scheme in 1765. The lake, produced by judiciously damming a small stream, and the parkland remains, but the hall was pulled down in the 1950s.

Changes in a Suffolk village can be seen in this 1967 view of Holbrook, in the Shotley Peninsula 6 miles from Ipswich. In the foreground is All Saints' Church, whose tower in common Suffolk fashion doubles as a porch. Not far away new houses are going up, and up the village street to the left of the picture a new estate is being developed. The name of Holbrook is known throughout Britain through the Royal Hospital School, a boarding school originally for the sons of officers and men of the Royal Navy and Royal Marines, which moved from Greenwich to new buildings in the parish in 1933; it lies on the other side of the valley off the bottom of the picture.

Kersey, whose heart lies on the slopes of a steep valley barely discernible from above, was one of the communities in the Babergh Hundred that flourished in the Middle Ages on the woollen cloth trade. St Mary's Church, which stands at the top of the hill on the southern side of the village centre, was being rebuilt when the Black Death brought work to a stop in the mid-14th century. Work did not begin again for half a century, and the tower was not finished until 1481. On the further side of the valley a curving hedgeline preserves the boundary of the Augustinian priory which once occupied the site of Priory Farm. Research has shown that the name 'Kerseys' for a type of woollen cloth probably did not originate from the village name, which means 'cress island'.

Framsden, which lies equidistant from Ipswich, Woodbridge and Stowmarket – it is eleven miles from all three – lies next to Helmingham, and much of the land in both parishes is owned by Lord Tollemache, of Helmingham Hall. The houses bordering the road in the foreground, with their little front gardens and extensive plots at the back, are estate cottages built by the Tollemaches. On the hill towards the top of the picture is Framsden Mill, a postmill built for miller John Flick in 1760 on a piece of land called 'The Overies' which he had bought the previous year. In 1836 it was bought by a John Smith, who modernised the mill, using the current developments in mill design to make it more efficient and easier to operate. It ceased work in the 1930s and was restored by a group of enthusiasts some 30 years later.

Heaps of scrap vehicles form one of the most prominent features in this 1973 photograph of Coldfair Green, a settlement in the parish of Knodishall near Leiston. This is the Sandlings area of Suffolk, which was at one time largely heathland; during the Second World War much of the remaining heath was brought under the plough, as seen at top right. The name Coldfair Green is said to be derived from a fair once held on the green each December.

Kelsale, just north of Saxmundham, must once have gained considerable advantage from its position on, or close beside, the main London–Yarmouth road. In this 1973 photograph the A12 runs in an almost straight line past the village, separating it physically from its twin parish of Carlton to the west. Beyond the church of St Mary and St Peter, with its churchyard avenues of lime trees, there is a surviving moat hidden by a belt of trees. This section of the Yarmouth road is now relegated to a B-road following the construction of the Saxmundham by-pass.

Modern roads tend to cut across the countryside with little apparent regard for existing landscape features. Taken on 13 June 1968, this photograph shows improvements being made to the A12 trunk road at Copdock and Washbrook, just to the south of Ipswich; the old road can be seen on the right passing through the village of Washbrook. Further changes have been made since with the construction in the 1980s of the Ipswich southern by-pass, part of the A14 trunk road from Felixstowe to the Midlands, and the whole of this section of the A12 is now dual carriageway.

In a scene of rural tranquillity, the round-towered All Saints' Church at Frostenden stands in relative isolation among the fields west of the A12 road between Wangford and Wrentham, with just Hall Farm nearby. At least the base of the tower is Saxon, but the rest of the building is 13th and 14th century. There are indications that when the church was built Frostenden was a port with a quay on a navigable river; but the river is now no more than a small stream and the sea is nearly 3 miles away.

In contrast, all is bustle as preparations are made for the Royal Show at Ipswich in June 1934. Ipswich Corporation extended its London Road trolleybus route to serve the showground, on land on which the Chantry Estate is now situated, and built an additional ten double-deck trolleybuses for the Royal Show service; the chassis for the new vehicles were made in Ipswich by Ransomes Sims & Jefferies. The large horse ring and collecting ring can be seen in the middle of the picture, with the cattle, sheep and pig pens in the foreground. The show, the 93rd held by the Royal Agricultural Society of England, was visited by the Prince of Wales (later Duke of Windsor) on 4 July.

46

Country Towns

Perhaps the best-known small market town in Suffolk is Lavenham, but this is not the Lavenham visited by thousands of holidaymakers today. This photograph, taken on 3 April 1929, bears evidence of a community that is self-sufficient and much less aware of being a magnet for tourists; there were then four butchers' shops, five grocers and four bakers as well as a variety of other shops in the town – and not one of them an antique shop. It all looks deserted at first glance, but there is washing on the lines and a wisp of steam comes from J.W. & F.W. Baker's steam mill in Prentice Street, where a team of horses stands waiting in the yard. Of the buildings in the middle of the Market Place, all but one have been cleared away since the picture was taken. Today it is usual to refer to Lavenham as a village, a sad reflection on the decline of what was once a thriving centre of the woollen cloth trade.

The market town of Stowmarket, seen here on 9 October 1928, received a commercial boost when the Gipping was made navigable up to the town in 1793. The malting trade was important to the town, and so was the brewery that can be seen just to the left of the church spire; India Pale Ale made there went downriver in iron barges in the 1840s to be exported to quench the thirst of British troops stationed out East. Central in this picture is the parish church of St Peter and St Paul, and St Mary; the second dedication is due to the fact that there were formerly two churches in the same churchyard.

Until 1934 the parish boundary of Stowmarket was the river, visible in the left foreground of this view of Stowmarket railway station (formerly in Stowupland) and the surrounding industrial area taken on the same occasion as the photograph opposite. The railway arrived in 1846 and the somewhat ornate station, hailed as 'one of the handsomest in the county', was designed by Frederick Barnes. Several sidings diverged from the main line to serve nearby maltings and other establishments, one passing through the building in the foreground before crossing the river by a bridge to reach premises on the town side.

Needham Market lies on the Gipping a few miles below Stowmarket, its origin being as a minor market town in the parish of Barking. Until the beginning of this century it was ecclesiastically no more than a hamlet of Barking with a 15th-century chapel-of-ease; it became a parish church only in 1901. The railway station, on the right of this pre-Second World War photograph, was another designed by Frederick Barnes; it has what might be the earliest subway beneath the lines. To the left are the mills of D. Quinton and Sons and maltings owned by Walter Clowes and Co.

Opposite: Like many of its neighbours in West Suffolk, Hadleigh had thrived in the Middle Ages on the woollen cloth trade; tenterframes were set up in the fields alongside the River Brett, which flows along the north and west sides of the town, and the river undoubtedly provided both power and water for fulling mills in which the woven cloth was cleansed and pounded to felt the fibres. In 1950, when this photograph was taken, there were still two cornmills on the Brett, Toppesfield Mill near the part-medieval bridge at the south end of the town and the other at the north end near the prominent gasworks; both fell victim to fire. A number of maltings, with their pyramidal kilns, are to be seen in the town, and close to one in Duke Street leading down to Toppesfield Bridge is the former silk mill of 1834, later used for the manufacture of coconut matting.

Cavendish, in the Stour valley 4 miles west of Long Melford, is visited by thousands of tourists who stare across the attractive green to the church, seen on the left of this 1970 photograph, and the old thatched cottages of Hyde Park Corner; these were restored after falling into decay, destroyed by a fire and then again rebuilt. The tourists then visit the museum established by Sue Ryder when she made Cavendish the headquarters of her Sue Ryder Foundation, set up to care for victims of wartime persecution and now providing homes for seriously handicapped people. The trackbed of the Stour Valley line, closed in 1966, can be clearly seen on the right.

Little more than 2 miles further up the Stour valley is Clare, which even today retains the street layout imposed when the Norman castle was built. The Stour Valley railway was still in operation when this picture was taken, and the number of freight wagons in the little goods yard below the castle motte seems to indicate a thriving traffic. The road to the station follows the curve of the inner defences. Beyond the confines of the old town new houses are being built on what had been farmland; later a large school was to be erected on the other side of the road to Cavendish, at the back of the row of houses bordering the road.

With an area of almost 17,000 acres (6,880 hectares) Mildenhall is Suffolk's most extensive parish. The town itself was in 1930 quite compact, with the houses grouped around St Mary's Church on three sides and the old market place just north-east of the church; as so often happened, a group of buildings encroached on the original market square, confining it to an elongated quadrangle. Down by the Lark, on the extreme right, are the big water mills belonging to Parker Brothers which not only ground corn into flour but provided the town with its first electricity supply. Work on the building of an RAF aerodrome began in 1934 on land to the west of the town; it is now a huge US Air Force base handling the world's largest transport aircraft.

Newmarket, lying astride the main road from London to Norwich, became linked with royalty in the reign of James I and soon became a centre of horseracing. It has been the capital of racing ever since. In this view, taken looking east-north-east across the town in 1969, the High Street, part of the A11 trunk road, runs obliquely across the middle of the picture. Park Paddocks and Tattersalls' sale ring, in which some of the world's most famous horses have appeared, can be seen to the right of the trunk road in the middle of the picture. The firm of Tattersalls was founded by Richard Tattersall in 1766 and soon began its association with Newmarket, sales being held in the High Street outside the Jockey Club rooms. They were transferred to Park Paddocks in 1870. Long Hill and Warren Hill can be seen at the top of the picture, with the railway line disappearing into the tunnel under the hill.

Haverhill was in 1929, when this photograph was taken, a town of just 4,000 inhabitants. Dominant in this view are the Chauntry Mills of D. Gurteen & Sons Ltd, 'makers of all classes of clothing for wholesale home trade & export; woollen goods in juvenile & men's; corduroys & moles, white drill, blues for mechanics & engineers, & shirts, gloves & leggings. . .'. The firm had grown to prominence at the beginning of the 19th century when it made smocks for agricultural workers; in 1879, when the town had a population of only 3,000, Chauntry Mills employed 2,500 men, women and young people, many of whom came in from the surrounding country areas each day.

In 1959 estates of new houses were being built by the Greater London Council on the outskirts of old Haverhill, which had been chosen for an overspill scheme that was to change the character of the town irredeemably. The 1955 agreement with the GLC was to expand the population to 10,000; then it was suggested the final figure should be 18,500, and then 30,000. The old town centre was quite unable to cope.

Great Cornard was no more than a scattered village with a population of around a thousand a mile or so from Sudbury until the Greater London Council conceived the idea of exporting some of its surplus population to Suffolk. The Pot Kiln estate, which took its name from the yard in which Hannah Hunt produced coarse earthenware in the mid-19th century, was built to house some of the overspill population, and Pot Kiln Primary School in the foreground was established to serve the new population. The land to the left of the picture was former chalk workings, and unfortunately the land on which the estate was built turned out to be riddled with old tunnels in the chalk, leading to serious fears of subsidence.

The small town of Brandon, in the Breckland, used to carry on a considerable trade in malt, corn and coal by way of the Little Ouse, which can be seen flowing from left to right across the photograph. The river forms the boundary between Suffolk and Norfolk. It was also a noted centre for the manufacture of gunflints, made from flint mined on the heath in the right background; at the time of the Napoleonic Wars this was a thriving industry, and it survived into the 20th century owing to the fact that natives in some parts of the Empire were allowed to own nothing more modern than flint-lock guns. The town's other industry was the dressing of rabbit skins whose fur was used by makers of felt hats; this trade suffered a downturn when myxomatosis struck the rabbit population in the early 1950s.

The centre of Halesworth has not changed markedly since this photograph was taken in 1969 except that through traffic has been taken by a new road passing along the right-hand side, allowing the Thoroughfare to be given over largely to walkers. St Mary's Church stands in the middle of the town on the site of a much earlier round-towered church; the present building is largely a product of the 14th and 15th centuries, expanded in Victorian times to accommodate a growing population. Both the railway station on the East Suffolk line, unusual in that part of the platform was made up of level crossing gates, and the former quay on the Blyth, made navigable up to Halesworth in the 1790s, are out of the picture to the right.

In the past Eye was a place of some importance, for its castle was the administrative headquarters of a large landowner, the Conqueror's henchman William Malet, and his successors. Today it is a quiet little place several miles off the main road, with a stylish Victorian town hall to remind its inhabitants of the days when it was a borough. There is new housing on the outskirts of the town and an industrial estate on the Second World War airfield, seen in the background of this picture, taken in 1964; Eye was one of the bases used by the US 8th Army Air Force for bombing raids on Germany and occupied Europe.

The East Suffolk railway line, opened in 1859, is the most prominent feature in this photograph of
Saxmundham taken on 25 July 1920. The arrangement of the station is somewhat odd, with the down
platform on the near side of the level crossing and the up platform on the far side. This was the junction for
the Aldeburgh branch, which can be seen curving away to the right at the top of the picture; the line has
been closed beyond Leiston but still operates for nuclear fuel trains as far as Sizewell siding. At the time the
photograph was taken the narrow High Street was part of the main road from London to Lowestoft and
Yarmouth, the A12, the town only being by-passed in quite recent years.

On the Waveney in the north-east of the county is the town of Bungay, seen here in a photograph taken in about 1920 from a low level above St Mary's Church, whose tower can just be seen at the bottom. Above the tower is the dome of the Butter Cross of 1689 surmounted by the figure of Justice – without the usual blindfold. Only one motor-car can be seen in this view, outside the Three Tuns Hotel. In the left background can be seen the printing works of Richard Clay, first established in the town in 1795.

Beccles lies on the Suffolk bank of the Waveney and gained the status of a minor inland port when Lowestoft harbour was opened and the river dredged. Possibly it regained that status, for at the time of the Norman Conquest the town was paying a fee of herrings. The unusual plan of the church, with a detached tower at the south-east corner of the churchyard, is due to the fact that it is built on top of the riverside cliff seen in the photograph, taken in 1928, rising from Puddingmoor; the ground at the west end of the church was too unstable to bear the weight of the tower, which never reached its intended height. To the right of the church tower can be seen the market place; over the years permanent shops have been built on the old market place, but narrow alleys between the buildings still replicate the alleyways between the rows of stalls.

Bury St Edmunds

Before the amalgamation of the two counties of Suffolk in 1974 Bury was the county town of West Suffolk and the administrative centre for an area that stretched from Newmarket to Hadleigh. In 1920, when this photograph was taken from a de Havilland DH9 – the lower wing can be seen at extreme left – the town retained much of the atmosphere it had had when in the 18th century it was the centre of social life for the gentry living in the countryside around.

The commercial centre of Bury is the Cornhill and Market Place. The photograph, taken from a low level in June 1920, makes it plain that the original market place was very much larger than the present one, several rows of buildings having been erected in the middle of the wide open space that was once given over to stalls. No doubt in the first place it was those stalls, assuming permanent form, that began the infilling. One of the alleyways between the stalls has become the narrow lane known as The Traverse.

An ecclesiastical and civic procession emerges from the 14th-century Abbey Gate and makes its way along Angel Hill towards the Cathedral on 9 October 1928, to celebrate the meeting of the Norman barons at Bury on 20 November 1214, at which they took an oath before the high altar of the abbey to compel King John to sign Magna Carta. Leading the procession are the Right Revd H. Hensley Henson, Bishop of Durham, the Right Revd Godfrey Whittingham, Bishop of St Edmundsbury and Ipswich, the Mayor of Bury, Mrs Greene, and the town mace bearers. At the far right is the front of the Athenaeum, designed by Francis Sandys as the town's Subscription Rooms. Even at this early date Angel Hill has become a car park.

Looking north across the Great Churchyard and the site of Bury Abbey in 1949, with St Mary's Church in the foreground. The Abbey, with the mummified corpse of St Edmund 'miraculously' reunited with its head, became a great centre of pilgrimage in the Middle Ages, the magnificent Norman Tower providing pilgrims with a suitably impressive entrance to the Abbey. St James's Church, which shares the churchyard, became the Cathedral of the new Diocese of St Edmundsbury and Ipswich in 1914.

Brewers Greene King have been in business since 1806, when William Buck and Benjamin Greene 'begged leave respectfully to inform the public that they will be ready by the first week in June, to execute any order they may be favoured with for Table Beer'. The Westgate Brewery that was pictured in 1974 did not all date back to the 19th century, for the brewhouse that forms the central feature of this photograph was built only in 1937–38. Opposite the brewhouse is the Georgian Theatre Royal, once used by the brewery as a barrel store but now back in use for the purpose for which it was built in 1819.

Out along the Sudbury road is what is now known as The Fort, all that remains of the early 19th-century Bury Gaol, closed in 1878. The radiating arms containing the cells have gone, the hub survives – it was the governor's residence. Also surviving is the forbidding frontage with its pedimented gateway above which were hanged many criminals, including the notorious William Corder of Red Barn fame.

Gibraltar Barracks was the depot of the 12th Foot, The Suffolk Regiment, now amalgamated with the Royal Norfolk Regiment to form the 1st Battalion, The Royal Anglian Regiment. It took its name from the fact that the 12th played a part in the Siege of Gibraltar, 1779–82, and so adopted the castle and key of Gibraltar as their cap badge. In 1959 there were still recruits drilling on the square

The central core of Bury remains, to some extent, as it was when laid out by Abbot Anselm more than 900 years ago; one of the buildings in this photograph is the Norman Moyse's Hall, dating from the late 12th century and among the oldest stone houses in the country. Although plans for comprehensive redevelopment of the area to the left of the photograph, taken in 1976, were thrown out there have been many changes in recent years, one of the more obvious being the use of the cattle market as a car park. Large new shop and business premises have replaced many of the more modest old buildings, although at 25 Abbeygate Street there is a chemist's shop occupying a building that has been associated with medicine and pharmacy for some 250 years. Such survivals are rare, and it is probably fair to say that the charming old town of Bury deserves more sympathetic treatment than it has had from the 'planners' in the past 50 years.

75

St Mary's Hospital began life as the Thingoe Union Workhouse, taking in paupers from the 50 parishes surrounding Bury; it also accommodated paupers from the town, the old Bury workhouse in College Street being used latterly only for 'vagrants', the official term for what are commonly termed tramps. The original building is of similar form to the Bury Gaol, with arms radiating from a central hub; it was enlarged in 1879 so that it could accommodate 380 inmates.

Bury has not by any means escaped the worst excesses of 'progress'. In 1976, the year in which this photograph of the northern outskirts of the town was taken, historian Norman Scarfe railed against 'our blurred suburbanised vision' which had resulted in the building of the 'concrete and neon by-pass (opened 1973) right across the slopes of former medieval vineyard in the east, with (against all planning principles) acres of housing and light industry immediately beyond that, cut off from the town by the motor-way'. From the air one sees very well what he means. Sancton Wood's railway station is at lower left, and by the beet sugar factory is an enormous roundabout giving access from the A45 (now A14) to the town by way of broad, curving roads and more roundabouts.

Ipswich

The heart of Victorian Ipswich, photographed on a January day in 1921, looking up from Queen Street towards Cornhill, with Brightwen Binyon's Corn Exchange of 1878–82 and the Town Hall of 1867–68 in the middle of the picture. Lloyds Avenue has not yet pierced the range of buildings on the north side of Cornhill and the electric trams have not yet given way to trolleybuses; surprisingly there is not a single tram to be seen. Ipswich was at this time a county borough and the county town of East Suffolk, with the county administrative offices at County Hall in St Helen's; the Town Hall was the centre of the borough administration and the headquarters of the borough police force, which had its station on the King Street side of the building.

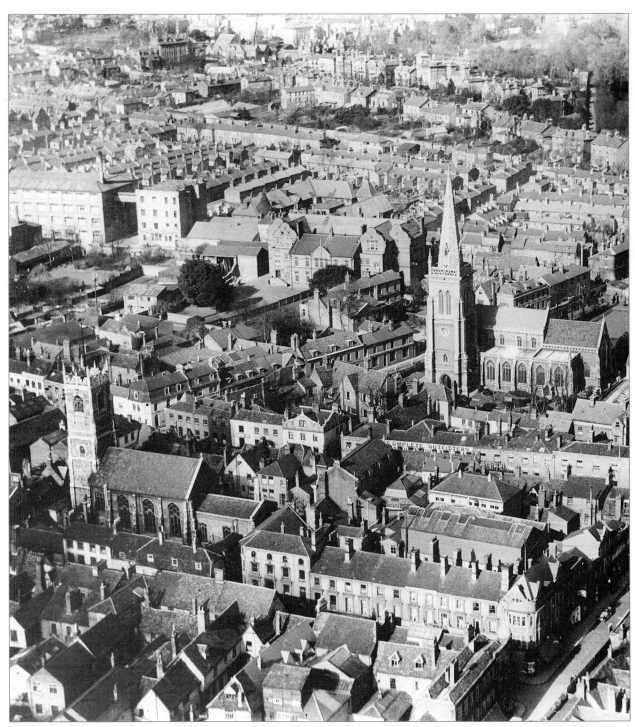

Two of the town's medieval churches, St Lawrence's and St Mary-le-Tower, can be seen in this view, taken in March, 1921. The latter, always considered the town's senior parish church, had been entirely rebuilt in Victorian times by R.M. Phipson, and the tower of St Lawrence's with its typically medieval flushwork is also a rebuilding of 1882; the original tower was by no means as high. Immediately to the left of the spire of St Mary-le-Tower is the council school fronting on to Tower Ramparts. Where the buses now pick up their passengers is a large malthouse, and beyond are streets of little houses where Crown Pool and the multi-storey car park now stand; in the distance are the much grander houses of Fonnereau Road.

St Margaret's Church and Christchurch Mansion, with the wooded slopes of Christchurch Park beyond, also seen in March 1921. Christchurch Mansion was given to the town by Felix Thornley Cobbold in 1895, and after some hesitation the Corporation acquired the parkland on behalf of the townspeople, with the lasting result that in spite of 20th-century development Ipswich retains a green lung within reach of the town centre. On St Margaret's Green several country buses, overgrown carrier's vans, await the time of their departure for Boyton, Charsfield, Clopton, Halesworth, Woodbridge and other places to the north and north-east of the town.

A development of the 1920s was the Racecourse Estate, built by Ipswich Corporation on the site of the old Ipswich racecourse on which the last flat race had been run in 1911. The first houses were occupied in 1921, and by the time this photograph was taken in 1930 the estate had a well-settled appearance. The layout of the estate, with the main roads radiating from a central hub like the spokes of a wheel, was hailed as a great improvement on the grid-like pattern of older housing areas. A 1930s handbook spoke of 'a well-conceived town-planning scheme that . . . studiously avoids the monotonies of English suburbia and the hideousness of ribbon development'.

Also taken in 1930, the photograph above shows the Gainsborough Estate, another Corporation housing area laid out in the 1920s. Beyond the houses is Ipswich Airport, then newly opened as a grass airfield with relatively few facilities. Aircraft at the airport in this period are seen in the picture below. Further on is the green-field site to which Ransomes Sims & Jefferies moved their works in 1950.

This view across the Wet Dock from the east reveals how a bend in the river was used to form the dock, the New Cut being dug to carry the water from the Gipping away to the sea. In the foreground are the works of Ransomes Sims & Jefferies and other industrial premises attracted to the dock area. Near the head of the dock is Stoke Bridge, built in the 1920s to replace the centenarian cast-iron bridge erected by Ransomes, and further upstream is Princes Street bridge leading to the railway station. Over Stoke, on the west bank of the river, is a mixture of industry and housing, with the railway locomotive depot at far left.

Another photograph of the dock taken on the same flight in 1930 shows the entrance lock opened in 1871 and the gasworks, including the first waterless gasholder built in Britain, erected in 1928. By this time railway sidings had replaced the old Promenade to the left of the lock that had been such a favourite Sunday morning walk for Ipswich residents in Victorian and Edwardian times.

The same area seen from a higher level, and 20 years later. The layout of the Wet Dock and the New Cut can be seen particularly well in this view, which also shows Ransomes & Rapier's Waterside Works at bottom left. The paddle steamers of the earlier views have been replaced by the *River Lady*, a former naval motor launch of the Second World War, and a similar converted naval vessel.

Shipping at South West Quay in the dock in 1973, the year work started on turning mudflats on the west side of the river into a new terminal. The swing bridge over the entrance lock was built in 1929 by Ransomes & Rapier, a corner of whose works can be seen on the far side of the New Cut; it took the place of an earlier bridge put in place in 1906. The aircraft's wingtip obscures the view of R. & W. Paul's Stoke maltings. The sight of three vessels at South West Quay would be unusual today, for expansion of the port downriver and on to the west bank has taken much of the trade from the old dock.

This view of Portman Road football ground and the cattle market taken in 1933 is of special interest as it shows also a part of the town centre that was greatly changed when Civic Drive and Franciscan Drive were cut through the area in the 1960s. Many of the houses on the extreme right were eradicated with the erection of the unfortunate Greyfriars development.

Many changes are apparent in this view looking across the southern part of the town centre towards the Orwell in July 1965. In the left foreground the hole for the Civic Centre underground car park is being excavated, Civic Drive is in course of construction, and the Greyfriars development is under way. In the right background is the Cliff Quay power station, commissioned in 1950 and demolished in 1994; people turned out in their thousands to see the three chimneys felled by explosives.

The underground car park and Civic Drive are complete in this photograph taken in June 1969, showing the whole of the town centre; Greyfriars is in being, and Franciscan Way discharges its traffic into the narrow St Nicholas Street, while close by the underground car park work has started on the foundations of the new Civic Centre to which local administration will before long be transferred from the Victorian Town Hall, seen near the centre of the picture. The area just above the underground car park is today used by the town's market, which has enjoyed a peripatetic life for almost 200 years. A new provision market opened in 1810 on the site now occupied by the Buttermarket shopping precinct and remained in use for much of the century until the market moved to the Corn Exchange; the market was moved to the bowels of the new Greyfriars development when that opened, then went to Tower Ramparts for some time, and with the building of Crown Pools was removed to the site seen here.

The town's road layout shows up starkly in this photograph which has Stoke Bridge and the river at the bottom and St Matthew's Street, Crown Street and St Margaret's Plain at the top. The old street pattern was largely that laid down in the Saxon period, with a few additions in Victoria's reign; the new roads, Civic Drive and Franciscan Drive, cut right through the western part of the town centre without regard for anything already existing. Such is the scale of the Greyfriars development that it dominates the scene; had the plans of the 1960s come to fruition there might have been many more buildings on a similarly massive scale, but the Government had second thoughts on its expansion scheme for Ipswich.

The Rope Walk area had been a labyrinth of 19th-century working-class streets, but slum clearance made way for the building of the Civic College, now Suffolk College, opened by the Queen in 1961. The open area to the left of the college buildings, in this picture of 1969 with just a dozen cars parked on it, is now the site of St Edmund House, accommodating the planning and other departments of the county council. The trees just beyond the college are in Alexandra Park; on the far side of the park is Grove Lane.

The old centre of Ipswich, with the Town Hall and Corn Exchange, together with the Head Post Office, and the new Ipswich, the Greyfriars development dwarfing St Nicholas's Church, in the background. Across the road from Greyfriars and next to the Unitarian Meeting House the site of the British Lion public house and other buildings is being prepared for the building of the startling glass-walled offices for Willis, Faber, Dumas, now known as Willis Corroon Plc. In the foreground Lloyds Avenue, a product of the early 1930s, tunnels through the buildings to reach the Cornhill.

On the same day that the previous photograph was taken, an Aerofilms photographer took this shot of the St Matthew's roundabout from above Berners Street. Civic Drive curves round past the Civic Centre, with the two office blocks of Guardian Royal Exchange Insurance (as it then was) on the far side of the road and a corner of Greyfriars on the edge of the picture. In the distance Princes Street runs straight towards the railway station. All that is missing from the new Ipswich is the Wolsey Theatre, yet to be built.

This vertical photograph shows Ipswich in 1979, north being to the left and Cornhill right in the centre, as it should be. For centuries the market for corn had been held right in the middle of town, and the Cornhill became in very truth the centre of borough administration; only in the 1970s did the idea strike root of moving the administrative centre to the edge of town, unbalancing the historic core of Ipswich.

Coastal Towns

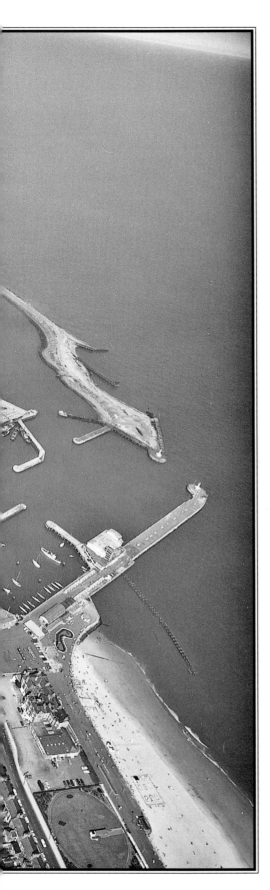

Lowestoft had been a place of trade for centuries, with ships landing their cargoes on the open beach – and some even being built on the beach – but it only became a port in the accepted sense in the 1830s when the harbour was constructed as part of a grand design promoted by Norwich merchants. The scheme was not a long-term success, and it was left to Sir Morton Peto to develop the outer harbour, and to the Great Eastern Railway to build the docks, used by the port's fishing fleets. The harbour and the railway yards are in the foreground of this photograph, taken in 1969 – before highways planners hit on the extraordinary idea of relieving traffic congestion by building a wide new road right through the built-up area to the left of the picture.

The new town of South Lowestoft was developed by Sir Morton Peto in the 1850s, using as his contractors the local firm of Lucas Brothers whose joinery works was on the site marked by a factory chimney in the background of this photograph, taken in June 1920. Until Peto purchased the land south of the harbour from the Improvement Commissioners for a mere £200 there was nothing but waste ground between the harbour and Kirkley, then a village quite separate from the town of Lowestoft. They were united when the Borough of Lowestoft was created in 1885.

A closer view of Sir Morton Peto's development, taken in May 1928. Along the Esplanade are the semi-detached villas provided for 'the better class' of resident – Thomas Lucas, of Lucas Brothers, lived in one of them – and behind them on Marine Parade are the fine terraces of 'second-class houses' designed by John Thomas – John Louth Clemence, architect and manager of Lucas Brothers' Lowestoft works, lived there. Peto provided the money for the building by Lucas Brothers of the new parish church of St John's, seen in the middle of this view; it was demolished in the 1970s.

In 1928 Kirkley Ham, on the south side of Lowestoft harbour, was badly silted; the building of larger ships by Richards Ironworks later necessitated dredging to enable vessels to be launched into the Ham. A Flower-class sloop of the Royal Navy's fishery protection flotilla, probably HMS *Godetia*, lies at moorings in the harbour, and a number of trawlers can be seen alongside the quay and moored in a group at right. In the background is Coke Ovens Junction, with the Norfolk & Suffolk Joint line to Yarmouth curving away to the north; the junction was so called because in the 1850s there had been coke ovens on the quay to supply the early coke-burning railway engines.

At the north end of Lowestoft is Belle Vue Park, with its pagoda-like shelter, and Sparrow's Nest, at the foot of this photograph taken in 1928. Sparrow's Nest had once been the summer residence of the Sparrow family, from Worlingham, near Beccles; the land on which Belle Vue Park was laid out had been the Bleach, where washerwomen spread their sheets to bleach in the sun. The bridge linking Belle Vue Park with Gunton Drive across the Ravine was given by William Youngman to celebrate Queen Victoria's golden jubilee; the corporation celebrated her diamond jubilee by purchasing Sparrow's Nest for the town.

The herring fishery benefited during the 19th century from the growth of new markets in the mushrooming industrial towns of the Midlands and from the construction of railways giving ready access to those markets, and by the end of the century the facilities provided by Sir Morton Peto were inadequate. In 1883 the Great Eastern Railway opened the Waveney Dock for the use of the fishing fleet, but the growth of the fishing industry was such that between 1902 and 1906 a second dock, seen here, was excavated to the north of the first; it was named after Lord Claud Hamilton, chairman of the Great Eastern Railway Company. The sea was constantly depositing shingle on the beach north of the harbour entrance, and the railway company established a ballast plant which provided material for use throughout its system; it can be seen particularly well in the picture on the opposite page.

The first Scots drifters have already arrived for the autumn herring fishing, and motor and steam drifters crowd the Waveney Dock in this view taken towards the end of October 1952. Twenty-five drifters line the quay; at the height of the season in November there might well be many more jostling for position to unload their catches. For the duration of the herring season the trawlers, which bring in white fish, have been banished to the Trawl Basin on the left.

The holiday village at Thorpeness was the brainchild of Stuart Ogilvie, a friend of J.M. Barrie, author of Peter Pan. From about 1912 onwards he developed the village with a variety of houses, several of them reproductions of historic buildings such as the Moot Hall at Aldeburgh. The Meare (so spelt at Thorpeness) to be seen at upper left was dug out from a marshland area as a boating lake for children; it is nowhere more than 3 feet deep. The holiday village concept was particularly suited to colonial civil servants and others working abroad who came home for occasional long leaves; shortly after the Second World War the company operating the village issued a brochure entitled 'Home Leave Houses at Thorpeness'. Water supply was by means of piston pumps operated by the windmill seen at upper right and on the opposite page. The postmill, which dates from 1803, was moved from neighbouring Aldringham in 1923 and converted to its new work by having a hole drilled down through the upright post on which the buck turns. Behind the mill is the House in the Clouds, a disguised water tower, now disused so far as water supply is concerned but still providing a most unusual residence.

Another postmill, this one at Aldeburgh, seen in a photograph taken from the open cockpit of a de Havilland DH9 in June 1920. Beneath the aircraft's wing is Aldeburgh station, terminus of a branch line from Saxmundham, now closed; the station site lies beneath a large roundabout. Just beyond the wingtip is the tower of the parish church of St Peter and St Paul in which the funeral service of Benjamin Britten was held; both Britten and Sir Peter Pears lived in Aldeburgh for many years, and it was here that Britten conceived the festival which has carried the name of Aldeburgh throughout the world of music and the arts. In spite of many of the events being staged in the concert hall at nearby Snape, it is still the Aldeburgh Festival.

Looking across the town of Aldeburgh from the south, also in 1920, with the river at the foot of the picture. On the bank is the former Grimsby fishing smack *Ionia*, which was turned into a houseboat and used for very many years as a holiday home. After having been a maritime town for centuries Aldeburgh became in the 19th century a seaside resort, though it never took to the leisure business so avidly as resorts like Clacton and Yarmouth.

A low-level photograph of Aldeburgh beach taken in 1959 showing the lifeboat at the head of its slipway. There have been lifeboats at Aldeburgh since 1851, when a boat was transferred from Sizewell, and from 1905 to 1959 there were two. The No 2 boat, Lucy Lavers, had recently been withdrawn when this picture was taken. The Aldeburgh station suffered two disasters, the first in 1859 when a self-righting lifeboat overturned, flinging its crew into the sea. More famous is the 1899 accident in which the lifeboat overturned, trapping some of the crew beneath it; six men out of 18 died that day, and another died three months later from the effects of the accident.

Woodbridge, seen here in 1962, was a trading port and minor shipbuilding centre in centuries when commerce depended very largely on the sea for transport. It lies several miles from the sea up the Deben, which can be seen in the middle distance, and as trade faded away yachting and pleasure boating filled the vacuum. The town's quays can be seen towards the right; closer at hand is the parish church of St Mary with its splendid 15th-century tower, the market place and the Elizabethan Shire Hall. To the right of the church is the site of a priory; the present gabled building on the site is now a junior school.

The seaside resort of Felixstowe is to a great extent a product of the 19th century predilection for sea bathing. A visitor in 1829 found that 'the place seems to be in a very thriving condition, many new houses have been built, & it promises ere long to become the fashionable resort of those who have money to throw away, & who cannot be satisfied with the comfort they find in their own houses'. By 1920, when this picture was taken, it had indeed developed into a thriving resort, and it has continued to expand since.

A half-mile pier was built at Felixstowe in 1905 to enable passengers to disembark from the Belle steamers which ran a regular service between London and the east coast resorts; an electric tramway was installed to carry visitors to and from the head of the pier at which the steamers berthed. This 1920 photograph shows the pier and the boating lake close to the landward end; it also shows that at the time development had not proceeded very far along Sea Road, though a rough road layout was already visible ready for the building that was soon to begin. Just inland from the pier is Tower Q, set into the cliff; it was one of a chain of martello towers built in 1808–10 to defend the coast against an expected French invasion.

At the north end of the new resort was a natural spring that was credited by doctors with being a cure for gout, not to mention also 'nervous prostration, depression, and overwork'. The Spa Pavilion, just at the back of the beach and seen here in a photograph of 1932, was erected in 1908–9 by a local builder and was opened on 25 June 1909, by Lord Claud Hamilton, chairman of the Great Eastern Railway, whose company was making great efforts to promote the resort. Behind it and a little to the right is the Cliff Hotel with its ornate verandas, built in 1906 for members of the Quilter family, which had run the nearby Bath Hotel for almost a quarter of a century; the Bath Hotel was burned down by Suffragettes in 1914.

Just beyond the Spa was the sumptuous Felix Hotel, with its 250 bedrooms, 20 grass tennis courts, two full-size croquet lawns and an 18-hole putting course. It was built by an Ipswich brewer, the Hon. Douglas Tollemache, who collaborated in the design with architect T.W. Cotman, and opened in 1903 after being three years in the building. The hotel was acquired in 1919 by the Great Eastern Railway as part of its well-ordered plan to develop the resort in conjunction with its rail services; in 1904 the company had introduced a two-and-a-half-hour non-stop service from Liverpool Street to Felixstowe. It will be noticed that the previous picture and this one form almost a continuous vista.

The Felixstowe shoreline looking north to the mouth of the Deben in 1972, showing how much development had taken place. It will be noted that building has filled the gap along Sea Road to the Herman de Stern Convalescent Home, at the bottom of the picture, and that housing reaches almost to Felixstowe Ferry. With fears of a rising sea level due to global warming the protection of such populated areas as this presents problems which have yet to be overcome.

Wartime neglect and storms had by 1954 reduced Felixstowe pier to little more than a stump, though the large dance hall built at the shore end in 1926 – not to be confused with the Pier Pavilion, the large building between the pier and the boating lake – still provided pier amusements. Beyond the narrow confines of the town development is spreading across what had been farmland; soon dock development would fill much of the land in the background.

The Fragile Coast

To seamen the Suffolk coast is a dangerous one because of the ever-changing sandbanks that provide a trap for the unwary. The coast itself is also changing, most noticeably as a result of erosion by the waves. Nowhere is this more apparent than at Dunwich, where a town that was of great importance in early medieval times has been washed completely away in the past 800 years. This view of Dunwich looking south-west was taken in 1949, with the village in the right foreground and the medieval Greyfriars just beyond. Much land has been lost in the past 50 years, and the clifftop has now reached the western ramparts of the old town; archaeologists keen to record what might soon be lost to the sea have been working on the site of the Greyfriars priory.

In summer the coast is alive with holidaymakers, some of whom enjoy the all-in entertainment of a holiday camp. In 1948, at a time when a week at a seaside holiday camp was the peak of many people's holiday ambitions and foreign travel was only for the most adventurous, a photographer flying along the coast between Yarmouth and Lowestoft took this picture of the chalets of a holiday camp at Hopton. The cliffs fronting the camp are Corton Cliffs; a narrow strip of land in the parish of Corton then cut Hopton off from the sea, but erosion has since placed Hopton firmly 'on Sea'.

In this 1965 photograph of Rogerson Hall at Corton the low December sun outlines the buildings in long shadows, and there is nobody to be seen on the paths linking the main buildings with the long ranges of 'chalets'. Nor is there anyone to be seen on the beach as the winter waves roll in at the very top of the picture.

Covehithe was once a seaport, but over the centuries the sea has eaten away at the cliffs and has taken much of the parish, threatening now to take also the part-ruined church. In this photograph, taken in 1954, the remains of a wartime 6-inch gun battery built in 1940 are dropping over the cliff; its guns had come from the cruiser HMS *Dartmouth*, built before the First World War and scrapped in 1930.

As the sea advances areas of freshwater like Easton Broad, 2 miles north of Southwold, are threatened with great ecological changes. The sea broke through during the great storm of 1953, and in this picture, taken in October 1954, efforts are being made to strengthen the narrow beach that divides broad and sea; to the north beyond Easton Wood there is flooding in the valley at Covehithe.

A new landmark arose on the Suffolk coast with the construction of the nuclear power station at Sizewell, east of Leiston, which was nearing completion when this photograph was taken in 1964. With Sizewell A feeding the National Grid, whose pylons stretch in a double line across the countryside, passing north of Ipswich, it was decided to build a second station, Sizewell B, an even more controversial power station than the first, and then a Sizewell C. Sizewell B is in operation, but the third station was cancelled. On the car park south of the nuclear site there arose a tearoom which the humorous proprietor christened Sizewell T; it serves generous portions of fish and chips, the fish landed on the adjacent beach by longshore fishermen.

At the mouth of the Deben is Bawdsey Manor, built by Sir Cuthbert Quilter from 1886 onwards. In 1936 the Air Ministry acquired the property and transferred to it the research being done at Orfordness by Sir Robert Watson Watt and his team on 'radio direction finding', later to be known as radar. In the grounds was installed the first of the Chain Home stations which played a vital wartime role.

Opposite: One of the wonders of the natural world is Orfordness, a 9-mile shingle spit which diverts the River Alde (or Ore) south from Aldeburgh. The ness itself appears in this 1972 photograph like a carbuncle sticking out to the east, just as it is portrayed on John Norden's map of 1601. From the air the course of old drainage channels long dried up are visible in the marshes towards the bottom of the picture.

On the other side of the Deben is Felixstowe Ferry, a hamlet much frequented by yachtsmen. Taken in 1972 at the same time as the previous picture, this photograph shows one of the martello towers, which is seen from the air to be ovoid (egg-shaped) and not circular; this shape was adopted as it was considered that cannon balls would be more likely to glance off. A bus is approaching from Felixstowe along the only access road. The ferry was operated for many years by Charlie Brinkley, who had lost his hand in a gun accident as a young man and had it replaced by a steel hook; when a particular piece of radar equipment was developed with a hook shape it was christened by the Bawdsey scientists the Brinkley Hook.

On the never-to-be-forgotten night of 31 January/1 February 1953, a combination of a north-westerly storm and spring tides caused the East Coast flood disaster that cost the lives of more than 300 people, 46 of them in Suffolk. At Felixstowe the sea attacked from two directions, the waves smashing the sea defences at the Manor House end of the town, as seen on these pages, and the tide sweeping in from the harbour, tossing residential caravans around like toys and reaching the eaves of prefabricated bungalows in the south end of the town; forty people died as the water engulfed their homes.

Caravans lie piled along the railway embankment and wreckage floats around the gasworks site a week after the flood. These photographs of the Beach Station area of Felixstowe were taken on 9 February as work began to drain the water away and make it possible for people to return to their homes; it was to be many more weeks before some of the evacuated residents could commence the miserable task of drying out their houses. Twenty-five years on contractors were working on a new sea wall that would protect not only the residential area of the town that had suffered so severely in 1953 but also the rapidly expanding dock complex.

Felixstowe Dock

Felixstowe Dock was the brainchild of the redoubtable 'Colonel' George Tomline, of Orwell Park, Nacton (he was honorary colonel of a Lincolnshire militia regiment) who had built up large landholdings in the Felixstowe area after acquiring Orwell Park in 1858. He envisaged that passengers coming by the railway, another of his schemes, would go on to Northern Europe by steamer after spending the night in the Pier Hotel, the square building at lower right. His ambitions did not reach fruition, however, and the dock had a hand-to-mouth existence in spite of industries such as the steam flour mills at lower left and the big maltings on the other side of the basin. This photograph, dated 1961, also shows at right the RAF station that was for many years home to the Marine Aircraft Experimental Establishment; a certain LAC Shaw, better known as Lawrence of Arabia, was stationed there at one time.

In 1951 the dock was bought by Gordon Parker, an agricultural merchant from West Norfolk who wanted his own port through which to export barley. He brought in a new and forceful management which soon began to build up new trades. When the Royal Air Force station which had been so much involved in the development of flying boats was closed in 1962 the dock company absorbed it, using the station's Titan crane, installed in 1933 to handle flying boats, to load heavy cargo including road vehicles. The three great hangars and the Titan crane can be seen in the lower part of this 1963 photograph.

The apron of the old air station soon gave way to the port's first container terminal, seen here in 1969. Containers which had proved a source of controversy and labour trouble at some other British ports were espoused wholeheartedly at Felixstowe, as other new concepts had been in earlier years. The tank farm seen in the left background had had its beginnings in 1911 when the Admiralty used the first tanks to hold oil fuel for its new oil-burning destroyers; by 1969 the tanks were being used for edible oils, industrial solvents and – the large tank at the back – liquid methane imported from North Africa.

New buildings spreading around the dock basin are evidence of a new vitality in this photograph taken in 1969; a large modern transit shed has taken the place of the old maltings, destroyed by fire a few years earlier. In the basin are no fewer than seven ships, and the number of lorry trailers lined up in front of the old dock company office provide an indication of the flourishing roll-on, roll-off traffic operated by the Transport Ferry Service ships.

A large ocean-going container ship, the *American Legacy*, berthed at the Landguard Terminal on 29 June 1972. So large a vessel could never have entered the old dock basin, but thanks to the dredging of a deepwater channel in the approaches it had no difficulty in berthing under the container cranes. The three great hangars and the barrack blocks of the air station have been turned to new uses. On the right containers are stored two high pending onward transmission either by road or rail.

With the growth of the port of Felixstowe new quays and new container terminals were built on what had been little more than wasteland. Here, in a photograph taken in July 1973, work is proceeding on the reclamation of a section of shore, with sheet piling being driven from a piling barge to form the quay heading and spoil being piped ashore from a dredger to build up the land surface. Felixstowe is now the country's biggest and busiest container port.

Shotley Gate and the naval training establishment known as HMS *Ganges* seen in 1967, nine years before the establishment closed. The training ship *Ganges*, a three-deck line-of-battle ship built in Bombay in 1821, arrived in Harwich harbour in 1899 and gave its name to the shore establishment some years later. In the Stour are two Trinity House lightships; there is a large Trinity House depot at Harwich, and it is normal for several lightvessels to be moored in the river in this vicinity while refitting or as standby vessels.

Industry

Much of Suffolk's industry naturally grew up to serve the interests of the county's farmers, either producing what was needed by them or processing their products. The chemical works of E. Packard & Co. Ltd at Bramford, on the Gipping a few miles from Ipswich, produced artificial fertilisers from imported phosphates brought upriver in the river barges which can be seen moored near the railway bridge at left and beside the works. In the right background of this view, taken in January 1921, is a large chalk pit with several kilns producing lime used to counter acidity of the soil, and on the river just above the works is Bramford Paper Mill, still so called from a former occupation but then grinding corn. Beside the mill is one of the Stowmarket Navigation locks, no longer in use since barges no longer went beyond the fertiliser works, which as a result of amalgamation in 1929 became part of the Fisons empire.

Taken on the same flight in October 1928 as the pictures of Stowmarket on pages 48 and 49, this photograph shows Hawks Mill on the Gipping at Needham Market and, at far right, the lock which enabled barges using the Stowmarket Navigation to pass upstream. The mill, since converted to a house, is a fine example of a late 19th-century watermill with a steam engine as auxiliary to the water turbine; the chimney can be seen at the back of the mill building.

Pakenham is the only village in Suffolk today with a windmill and a watermill both in working order. The windmill, seen here in 1958, has been owned and operated by the same family since 1885. Like Hawks Mill at Needham Market, the windmill had a steam engine as auxiliary power, though this was replaced by a Ruston & Hornsby oil engine in 1931. As can be seen, the windmill does not stand in isolation; among the ancillary buildings is an old railway carriage serving as an office and sack store.

Large maltings grew up in close proximity to the railway during the second half of the 19th century in order to take advantage of railway carriage of malt to the big breweries in London and Burton-on-Trent. This complex at Bury St Edmunds had its own siding; the disadvantage of this being on an embankment was overcome by having covered bridges leading from the maltings to the siding. On the other side of the line is a large timberyard and sawmill operated by the Eastern Counties Timber Co. Ltd. The railway line leaving the Ipswich line and curving away to the north is the Thetford line, from which passenger services were withdrawn in 1953; the line closed entirely seven years later.

Close to the centre of Bury St Edmunds was the St Andrew's Works of Robert Boby Ltd, manufacturers of seed cleaning machines and equipment for the malting trade, including the large-wheeled barrows always known as Boby carts. Robert Boby had set up in business as an ironmonger in the 1850s, and within a few years was manufacturing agricultural implements on the St Andrew's Street South site. The firm has now gone and the works has been cleared away; the only building to survive is the one on the left with three round-topped windows in the gable end, re-erected at the Museum of East Anglian Life in Stowmarket, where it houses steam engines and displays of bygone local industries, including Boby's.

The beet sugar factory at Bury St Edmunds was relatively new when the photograph above was taken in 1930; it had been built in 1925 for processing beet from Suffolk farms. It is served by a siding from the Ipswich to Ely main line, for much of the beet arrived from the farm by rail in the early days; a small shunting engine belonging to the British Sugar Corporation can be seen standing near the junction with the main line. The annual campaign was in full swing when the smaller photograph was taken in December 1966. The column of steam hanging over the factory when processing is being carried out serves as a landmark for many miles around.

Constructed in the mid-1920s at around the same time as the Bury St Edmunds factory, the Ipswich sugar factory at Sproughton is seen here in a photograph taken in June 1930. The first of the British Sugar Corporation factories was built at Cantley in Norfolk in 1912, and Bury and Ipswich were among the next batch to come into operation. Much of the machinery for these factories had to be imported from Holland, though as the campaign to produce British sugar from beet gathered momentum firms like Cocksedge & Co. in Ipswich began producing sugar processing machinery. In the foreground can be seen one of the locks on the Gipping, still working at this date.

Cement was being produced in Suffolk in the 19th century, George Mason having a works on the bank of the Deben at Waldringfield. In 1912 Mason moved to a new works employing modern rotary kilns close to the village of Claydon and right beside the Norwich–Ipswich–London railway line. Both the raw materials needed, chalk and clay, were obtained close at hand from pits in Great Blakenham. By the time this photograph was taken in 1971 the works had become part of Blue Circle Industries, but the address of the factory is still Masons Works, Claydon.

Before the First World War the British Diesel Company was set up to manufacture engines of the type designed by Dr Rudolf Diesel, their factory being built on what has become the Hadleigh Road Industrial Estate at Ipswich. Dr Diesel was on his way to Ipswich to visit the site when he disappeared from the Great Eastern Railway steamer *Dresden* on 26 September 1913. The firm was later taken over by Vickers-Petter, who eventually transferred production to one of their own plants in the Midlands. This 1930 photograph also shows the infant bacon factory of Harris (Ipswich) Ltd sandwiched between the two railway lines to Norwich and to Lowestoft. In the left background can be seen the tannery of W. & A.J. Turner (Ipswich) Ltd and the tower of a windmill that stood behind the houses in Bramford Road.

The Waterside Works of Ransomes & Rapier, builders of the first railway in China, seen in 1928. The firm came into being in 1869 when the original Ransomes company needed more room to expand its agricultural implement department to take advantage of the booming export trade and decided to turn the railway materials department into a new company; Richard Rapier (later Sir Richard) had been manager of that department. In this 1928 view two of the river steamers operated by the Great Eastern Railway between Ipswich, Felixstowe and Harwich can be seen alongside the landing stages in the New Cut. Beyond them are the maltings, now being converted into a business centre.

Opposite: In the 1950s Ransomes Sims & Jefferies moved to a new works built not far from the airport on the outskirts of Ipswich, where they continued with the manufacture of agricultural implements, grass machinery and electric trucks. The new Nacton Works had a connection to the Felixstowe branch, which can be seen running across the middle of the upper photograph, taken in 1969. The works has now become part of an extensive business park. On the other side of the line is the Suffolk Showground which became the permanent home of the Suffolk in 1956. The lower picture shows the old Orwell Works, home of the firm from 1849 until the move.

Richard Garrett set up in the village of Leiston in 1778 as an edge tool maker, with just a single horse to power the grindstone. Succeeding generations of the Garrett family developed the business into one of the world's leading manufacturers of agricultural implements and steam engines. By the time this photograph was taken in 1920 Leiston Works filled the whole area between Main Street and Cross Street and the firm had expanded to a new works known as Station Works, part of which can just be seen at top left. As the company progressed, so Leiston grew into a small industrial town in the heart of rural East Suffolk, some of the houses being built by the Garretts for their employees.

The printing trade became established in the Waveney Valley in the 18th century, but the earliest records of printing in the county go much further back, to the 16th century. This photograph of William Clowes & Sons' printing works at Beccles was taken in 1935, more than 60 years after the London printers had taken over the Beccles business of Crisp and Moore. The story of this works can be traced to the business of William Lenny, whose premises in the New Market at Beccles were acquired by Read Crisp in 1844.

The fishing industry at Lowestoft naturally attracted food processors to the town. This is the Co-operative Wholesale Society's canning factory in Waveney Drive, seen in 1928 when much of the surrounding area remained marshland. The factory was being built for Maconochie Brothers, who had been operating in Lowestoft since the 1870s, but before it was complete the firm decided to pull out of Lowestoft and to concentrate the business on its other canneries. Herrings were among the foodstuffs canned in the Lowestoft factory.

The most easterly gasworks in Britain was at Lowestoft, close to Ness Point, here photographed on a spring day in 1939. The original gasworks on the site had been erected in 1837 by James Malam, a pioneer gas engineer who was responsible for a number of other similar installations in East Anglia in the years between 1824 and 1840. They were taken over in 1853 by a local company which also supplied the town with water.

Eighty Years of Aerial Excellence

Aerofilms is a thriving commercial enterprise with a fleet of three aircraft fitted with state-of-the-art cameras. The company remains at the forefront of new technology in the sphere of aerial photography and surveying and is committed to the constant renewal of its aerial archive.

The Aerofilms library today holds over two million aerial photographs, dating from 1919 to the present day. The major part of the collection is taken up with UK photography. This includes historic black and white and modern colour photography which captures the face of Britain in the twentieth century. The archive also includes a fascinating collection of international aerial photography from the 1950s and '60s covering the Americas, Europe, Asia, Antarctica and Africa, and the Mills Collection, a unique record of Victorian London.

The Aerofilms collection comprises both vertical survey photography and oblique photography. Vertical photography has many uses, including mapping, surveying and land use. Oblique photography is excellent for display or publishing purposes. All photography is available as photographic prints, transparencies or scanned as digital files on cd-rom. Map accurate, rectified imagery is available through Aerofilms' Orthophoto Department.

All existing photography is easily available from the Aerofilms library. Details of specific areas of interest can be faxed or posted and a free search will be carried out for relevant views. For clients with exact specifications Aerofilms can be commissioned to take new oblique or vertical photography at competitive prices.

Aerofilms is currently in the midst of a project to provide complete aerial photographic coverage of England ready for the next millennium. The Millennium Aerial Photographic Survey (MAPS) by UK Perspectives will be captured in 1999 at 1:10,000 scale and produced digitally to a mapping specification to become the definitive base line data set.

AEROFILMS
LIMITED

Phone: 0181 207 0666
Fax: 0181 207 5433
Email: library@Aerofilms.com
Gate Studios Station Road Borehamwood Hertfordshire WD6 1EJ